The Book of Alpha

30 Rules I Followed to Radically Enhance My Confidence, Charisma, Productivity, Success, and Life

David De Las Morenas

ISBN-13: 978-1494886110

ISBN-10: 1494886111

Buyer Bonus

Thank you for buying *The Book of Alpha*. To get your free gift, go to **www.HowToBeast.com/Masculinity-Mistakes** and download *Masculinity Mistakes*. This eBook details the top 7 mistakes guys make that prevent them from becoming an alpha male.

Contents

My Story

Hi, I'm David.

Just three years ago I set out on a quest that transformed me – one that continues to transform me. It was as if my eyes were opened to an entire dimension of the world that I didn't know existed. I'd finally begun my metamorphosis – from boy to man.

Looking back, I was lost. I didn't know it, but I was lost nonetheless. I was your average college bro who did well in class, pulled stupid pranks with his friends, and got drunk on the weekends – sometimes getting laid in the process. We thought we ruled the world. We also thought the Boston University campus was the world.

And why wouldn't we? We had all accomplished every life mission we had ever been tasked with. Beginning in grade school – I got good grades, passed my classes, dominated the high school basketball team, and was accepted to a respected university. By the end of my senior year, I had lined up a solid job with a software company. Hell, I was crushing it – most kids weren't even finding work *in this economy.*

But after the graduation ecstasy wore off, I faced a harsh reality. My life was boring, my job wasn't fulfilling, I had no sense of purpose, I wasn't getting laid, and I didn't have much confidence. I was a long shot away from being anything close to an alpha male. Yes, I was making and saving money, but given the circumstances I found little gratification it that.

I was living in a continuous cycle of waking up, commuting to work, being there for 9 hours, commuting home, going to the gym, watching TV, and sleeping – then rinse and repeat. What was the next milestone – a promotion, maybe? Society, and my parents, had set no further expectations of me. I was lost.

I knew I had to find a way out – and I did. Since then I've quit my nine to five job (only to have them offer me a part-time position working whenever I want – from home), followed my passion for fitness and started working as a personal trainer for a respected gym, written and published two books (one of which is an Amazon best-seller), and had tremendous success with women – even finding one that's been a pleasure to date for the past 6 months. More importantly, I developed a beaming sense of confidence, charisma, and a strong body in the process – in short, I began to take on many characteristics of the alpha. I don't tell you all of this to impress you, but rather to impress upon you the value of the various tools, habits, virtues, and hobbies I will share with you in this book – the rules I followed to make this transformation.

Over the course of the last three years I've experimented with a large number of habits, activities, lifestyle changes, and hobbies. Some of them were nothing more than time wasted. But others had incredible benefits, and I can honestly attribute my entire transformation to the use of these tools.

And so I finally decided to analyze their effectiveness and consolidate them into a book – this book. Inside you will find a series of rules that I discovered after viewing the same patterns and effects over and over again – both in my life, and in the lives of close friends and family members.

I find that concise and actionable advice has been the most valuable to me, so I'll treat you with the same respect. Each of the following chapters represents a particular rule, my experience with it, the lesson I learned from applying it, and a step-by-step list explaining how you can take action. The book is laid out chronologically, in the order that I encountered and applied each rule. I will do my best to give credit to all those who acted as mentors to me on this journey – be they friends, authors, or otherwise.

What is Alpha

Before delving in to my journey and the rules I followed to transform my life and become alpha, I think it's wise to examine exactly what the term alpha means. Below are the most common definitions of the word.

1. *(noun)* the first letter of the Greek alphabet (A, α).
2. *(noun)* the first one; the beginning.
3. *(adjective)* being the highest ranked or most dominant individual of one's sex.

The third definition is the one that we will deal with in this book. This is the definition people refer to when they use the term *alpha male.* Yet I find that it commonly carries a negative connotation. It's often used to denote an asshole or someone who is overtly trying to assert their dominance – and this is where I must step in and make a critical distinction.

The man who consciously tries to dominate his group or the environment around him is not alpha. He desperately wants to be, but he doesn't have the confidence or the integrity necessary to embody this desired state. This yearning and sense of inadequacy manifests itself in a variety of aggressive, disrespectful, and unintelligent actions. He stares down other men on the street with the hope of intimidating them. He's loud and quick tempered, with both his friends and strangers. He constantly tries to prove his manliness through cheap shows of aggression. None of this is alpha.

The real alpha male is confident, charismatic, physically strong, experienced, and successful. More importantly, he doesn't feel the need to prove himself or show off any of these characteristics. He carries himself in a calm, cool, and collected manner. His presence alone demands respect – he doesn't need to do so verbally or physically. He's a truly dominant and respected individual.

The rules laid out in this book are meant to serve you on your journey to becoming a true alpha male, not the immature, attention-whoring counterpart. Please, bear this distinction in mind as you make your way through the following pages.

How to Read and Use This Book

While this book can certainly be read in one or two sittings, it contains far more advice that can be realistically digested and acted upon in such a small timeframe. I encourage you to read one or two chapters at a time. Alternatively you can plow through the whole book quickly, and then make your way back through a second time, little by little. In fact, this is probably how I would do it. It will give you a solid grasp of the big picture, and also allow you to choose particular areas to focus on for your second read.

After reading each chapter, I ask that you take some time to reflect on each step included in the *Take Action* section. Some of the chapters' activities can be completed in mere minutes, while others demand more time and energy. Rushing through the steps will not produce optimal results.

Keep in mind that I applied all of the rules and lessons included over about two years' time – and I'm still working on many of them today. Personal transformation and growth takes time. The fire can definitely be sparked in an instant, but the journey is one that lasts until you die. If reading this book can provide you that spark, or even just a slight push of momentum in the right direction – I will be extremely proud and honored to have served you in your journey to alpha.

Good luck and much love,

David

Chapter 1
How to build a strong body

The resistance that you fight physically in the gym and the resistance that you fight in life can only build a strong character.

- Arnold Schwarzenegger

My Experience

I had spent my junior year of school studying in Madrid. While I was there I worked as an intern for a medium-sized software company located just outside of the city. They specialized in mobile application development and domain security. My co-workers were private people, and their behavior was borderline passive aggressive. The only redeeming quality of the place was Fernando, my cubicle neighbor.

The day I started working there, Fernando was in charge of getting me up to speed. Not realizing I was an intern, he delved directly into explaining high level software engineering workflows and processes. I sat there clueless, but didn't say a word. At the end of his two hour lecture, I finally broke it to him that I was an intern there, only temporarily, and my primary job would be translating documentation. We laughed, and became fast friends.

Fernando was an interesting guy with deep passions for cars and lifting weights. I think those are literally the only two topics we ever talked about, with the exception of girls and sex every once in a while. Regardless, he was being coached by a professional bodybuilder, and was in the midst of a bulking cycle. For those of you who don't know, bulking is when you eat to gain weight, with the intention of putting on muscle and getting stronger.

I watched in awe as a nerdy computer programmer ate insane amounts of food and packed on slacks of muscle in front of my very own eyes. I was hooked, and spent nearly all of time at work researching bodybuilding websites - *I wanted to get big.*

I found a basic routine and signed up for the *Ayuntamiento* gym near my host family's house. Actually, I paid like 3 euros each time I went, because it was cheaper than a membership - go figure. This was a public gym, and all of the weight lifting equipment was about 300 years old. But it was my first real gym experience. I had dabbled with P90X the previous year, but gave it up because it made me feel like a soccer mom trying to lose weight.

I had no idea what I was doing, but I was hooked. I started to see changes in my body and my friends and family gave me compliments left and right. When I finally got back to Boston for the summer, I had plans to step up my game. I joined a nicer gym and selected a new routine.

Fast forward one month. I'm at the YMCA getting ready to attempt a new max on every bro's favorite lift - the bench press. The routine I'm following forces me to increase the reps and weight at a pre-determined pace, and this week will determine whether or not I move up in weight or not. My heart is racing and my palms are sweaty. I position myself under the bar, lift the weight from the rack, and start pumping away. Twelve reps later - I'm in heaven.

After only one month of being on this new routine, I've increased my strength by more than I did in the six months I spent lifting abroad combined. I un-rack the weights and walk over to my next destination like my nuts are the size of bowling balls. *I own this place.*

Over the course of the next few years I've continued to follow proper routines, build loads of muscle, cut fat, and get way stronger.

Rule 1: Lift the Weight

Building a strong body is an essential part of being alpha. Exercises like curls and triceps extensions don't build true strength; big movements like squats and deadlifts do. If you want to look good with your shirt off, and have the strength to back yourself up, you need to follow a proper routine. The effort you put in at the gym won't translate into real results if you don't. Furthermore, properly programmed routines will ensure a balanced physique and develop good posture.

Take Action

1. Pick one of the two routines below.
2. Search YouTube for video demonstrations of all of the exercises, so that your form is on point.
3. Do it.

All Pro's Beginner's Routine - This is the routine I used at the YMCA on that fateful summer day. It involves doing the same seven exercises three times per week.

Link:
http://forum.bodybuilding.com/showthread.php?t=1550094
23

StrongLifts 5x5 - This is another great option. You alternate between two different workouts, and only do three exercises each time you're at the gym. It sounds easy, but don't be fooled - these exercises are no joke, and they work every muscle in your body.

Link: http://stronglifts.com/stronglifts-5x5-beginner-strength-training-program

Neither of these routines includes a large variety of different exercises. The ones they do include, however, are the basis of every bodybuilder and power lifter's workout regimen. They work a lot of different muscles at once, and require you to develop good posture to perform them effectively – and therein lies their magic.

Chapter 2

Why learning game is necessary to attract hot women

Things may come to those who wait, but only the things left by those who hustle.

- Abraham Lincoln

My Experience

Post-graduation reality was starting to kick in. I was hanging out at my parents' house all day, every day – just waiting for my new job to begin. The most potent side-effect of this brutal transition from college fantasy life to whatever I was getting into was undoubtedly the lack of women – the lack of sex.

It was frustrating knowing that I wouldn't be moving back into a horny, college girl infested apartment come September. I'd have to work to catch my own game.

It was the morning of my family's departure to Spain – we go every year to visit family. As I'm looking for a movie to watch on my iPad to alleviate the boredom of a seven hour flight, my phone rings. It's my cousin. After we explain pleasantries, I express my frustration, "dude, I'm so sick of not getting any ass... UGGHHH! By the way do you know any good movies I can download for my flight?"

His response changed my life. He suggested that I try reading a book – *Make Her Chase You*. It was by Tynan, a nerdy guy who moved into a house full of professional pickup artists and began slaying women left and right. I was skeptical at first –

do I really need to read a silly pickup manual to get laid!? Also, I don't read. I literally used Spark Notes for every single book in high school and college – and when there were no Spark Notes available, I would pray. But this book was only two dollars for the kindle and we were on our way out the door. I bought it.

I cruised through the whole book on that flight. It's not that long – please, don't be impressed. However, it did turn on multiple light bulbs inside my head. It was one of those situations where every technique the author suggested was somewhat obvious, but I knew I wasn't applying it on a consistent basis.

Keep in mind during college I never had a girlfriend. My love-life was without love – it was more like a series of drunken flings. I have to admit – my game was weak. Worse actually – it was borderline non-existent.

But this book had given me the push needed to accept the fact that hot girls wouldn't be showing up at my doorstep anytime soon. They wouldn't be falling into my lap at the bar either. I accepted the fact I'd need to seek them out and approach them, or give up on sex – clearly not an option.

Approaching women wouldn't be easy, it's not something I was comfortable doing – few men are. But it was a necessary evil. You'll read more on my actual experience approaching girls later in the book.

Rule 2: Approach Women

Your list of potential mates won't grow any larger if you don't meet new women. This is a fact. Sure, you can turn to online dating or hope for social introductions. But the average quality of women you find online is decidedly lower, and your friend may never introduce you to a hot, single girl who wants your nuts. As an alpha male, you should be able to find and attract your own women. Also, approaching signals confidence – and this puts you one big step ahead of every other chump out there.

Yes, there are many other characteristics that pickup artists teach, but I find that most of them are gimmicky. I've heard many friends who've entered into the pickup community admit that if the only change they made was to approach more women, their success rates would've increased at nearly the same pace.

Take Action

Below are a few activities to get you used to approaching cute girls.

1. Ask 10 strangers for the time.
2. Ask 10 strangers where the nearest coffee shop is.
3. Ask 10 girls you find attractive for the time.
4. Ask 10 girls you find attractive where the nearest coffee shop is.

Additionally, I recommend the following two books on game if you want to learn more about the whole process of seduction.

Make Her Chase You by Tynan – This is by far the most down-to-earth material I've ever encountered on the subject. It's also the first pickup book I read, and it served as a wonderful introduction for me.

Bang by Roosh – I read this later on. It's more of a textbook approach to getting better at approaching and attracting women. The writing is superb, and it answers nearly every question you can think of. Roosh also wrote *Day Bang,* a sequel of sorts that focuses on gaming girls during the day (i.e. not at bars or clubs).

Chapter 3
How to learn or enhance any skill

There is nothing noble in being superior to your fellow man; true nobility is being superior to your former self.

- Ernest Hemingway

My Experience

After reading Tynan's book, I began following his blog (www.tynan.com). I was surprised to see that it was far more focused on self-improvement than pickup. One of his most recent posts mentioned a book – *Ikigai* by Sebastian Marshall.

"Hell," I figured, "I just plowed through one book and loved it – why not try another?"

Ikigai was distinct from the recent pickup material I'd read. First of all, it was over 300 pages. I would've laughed in your face if you gave me a 300 page book just a few weeks earlier. But this reading thing was new to me. My reading-confidence was through the roof, and I had a few more weeks to kill before starting the new job.

The book dealt with everything from productivity and achieving to history and strategy. Every few pages I would have an epiphany about something that I should begin doing to improve my life. It was by far the most motivating thing I'd ever experienced. I was feeling guilty for not trying to accomplish bigger goals in my life. All of a sudden, the software job I was about to begin didn't feel like the Holy Grail of life achievements. *I wanted more – a lot more.*

I clearly remember one of the more striking passages in the book. Sebastian calls out all the self-help gurus that passionately declare, "You can do anything, be anything, have anything!" That's bullshit, and we all know it. He points out that in life some things are zero sum games, and others are positive sum. The zero sum games are the ones that can be impossible to win. Referencing the NBA as an example, he says, "hard work, hustle, discipline might not be enough to play NBA-level basketball. Because there are only so many spots... So maybe you can't be an NBA player. Because there's somebody that'll work just as hard as you but also might have been born taller, or put on denser muscle, or has a higher vertical jump even after you've trained like crazy on it." As a lifetime basketball player, this struck home with me.

He continues to give examples of positive sum games that anyone can *win* at – science, art, and business, to name a few. When you do a good job at any of those things it doesn't take a spot away from someone else, like in the NBA. There's no hard limit to good business or quality art. He's quick to note, "That doesn't make it easy. But if you hustle long and hard enough, you should be able to break though if you're playing a positive sum game." That's just one example, but the entire book oozes this positive *get off your lazy ass and do something big* mentality.

Honestly, the experience of reading *Ikigai* just might be single-handedly responsible for igniting the transformation that began to take place in my life – the transformation this book is all about. Before I knew it, I went on a reading spree. I flew through books on productivity, goal setting, creativity, conversation, business, entrepreneurship, game, and just about any other area I could improve on.

Even though I wasn't accomplishing anything spectacular at that moment, the sense of purpose and determination that reading these books gave me was undeniable. I felt enlightened – like a new man. I was ready to crush the world underneath my very feet.

Rule 3: Improve Yourself

Alpha males are constantly growing. Rather than stagnating and living life on auto-pilot, they strive for greatness – for consistent self-improvement. It's the most noble and virtuous thing a man can strive for. It will improve your outlook on life, your position in it, and allow you to add more value to the world.

Take Action

1. Pick an area in your life you want to improve (girls, business, investing, conversation, sales, productivity, writing, etc.).
2. Search Amazon for a book on that subject.
3. Read it. Or just read *Ikigai* by Sebastian Marshall – it worked for me.

Chapter 4
The most important thing a man can do to live a fulfilling life

The important thing is that men should have a purpose in life. It should be something useful, something good.

- Dalai Lama

My Experience

"Are you ready?" my boss asks.

"Yes, let's go," I reply, and we head into a small conference room nearby. Today is my three month review. For those of you in the corporate world, I imagine you are very familiar with these wonderful and fabulous things.

I'm nervous, and having a hard time maintaining eye contact with my boss. I've only been here for a brief stint and everything is new to me. Nearly every day has been a race to familiarize myself with the basics of the various applications our company develops, or an attempt to configure them for a variety of client implementations – all while trying to learn two or three new software languages at the same time. I don't know what there is to review – I haven't accomplished anything yet.

Item by item, we go down a checklist of requirements necessary for advancing to Solutions Engineer II (I'm currently level 1). We check off maybe 10 percent of the items. *Holy shit!* I think to myself, *this is going to take a long time.*

At the time I was listening to an audio book – *The Luck Factor* by Brian Tracy. I highly recommend listening to audio books if you have a hard time reading, a long commute, or just find it convenient. This particular audio book is the essence of self-improvement. I listened to it every morning while driving to work, and arrived ready to beast through any challenge my boss threw my way. It revolves around the idea that there is no luck (in the traditional sense), and encourages you to set goals, take action, and use a variety of other tactics to bring success into your life. You should really listen to it.

That day, I decided to set a goal to achieve the promotion within three months. This was a very short period of time given the variety of skills I had to learn and the vast experience I had to accumulate in order to achieve the promotion. But I was determined. I threw everything I had at it, and made it my mission to see it through. I did everything in my power to focus my time at the office on the relevant items I had discussed with my boss. When I got home each night, I'd review my progress and prepare for the following day.

During this time I noticed something crazy. I was far happier than I'd been the first three months on the job. I woke up every day with a deep sense of purpose. I was directing all of my energy towards a particular outcome, and every time I accomplished a milestone that brought me closer, I felt like a king. People around the office were beginning to take notice. "David," one of my co-workers told me when most of the office was out to lunch, and we were preparing our meals in the kitchen, "Roger [the head of our department] told me you're learning everything very fast – faster than anyone in the history of our department." *Damn*, I thought – *it feels good to be a gangster.*

I felt so proud. This simple statement verified that my hard work was paying off, and I was on the right track to earning my promotion.

Rule 4: Have a Mission

Have you ever heard the expression *a man on a mission?* It's an undeniable trait of any alpha male. As men we have a deep need for purpose. Without a purpose we feel lost, depressed, and anxious. The funny thing is – it doesn't matter exactly what the purpose is. As long as you have something to direct your masculine energy and daily efforts towards, this need for purpose will be fulfilled – and you will radiate this sense of purpose and drive to the external world.

Take Action

1. Choose something that you want to accomplish in the next few months (any shorter and it's too easy; any longer and it can be demoralizing when you don't see any progress).

Examples: Get a job, run 5 miles, complete a programming course on CodeAcademy.com, write a short eBook and publish it on Amazon.com, start a WordPress blog, complete a Tough Mudder race, take a martial arts class, go on a date with a cute girl, learn the basics of a foreign language, hike a mountain, take a trip to Colorado (or anywhere, but I want to snowboard in Colorado at some point), etc.

2. Create an image in your mind of exactly what it will look and feel like once it is accomplished (this is important – it needs to be explicitly clear, so that you know for sure when it's done).
3. Choose a specific completion date. This is only something to

aim for – don't be anal.

4. Write it down, and look at it every morning going forward to remind yourself. Studies have shown that those who write their goals down on paper experience an exponentially higher success rate.

Example: I will write and publish an eBook. By February 1st it will be live on the Amazon.com bookstore for Kindle.

Chapter 5
How to be fearless

The primary thing when you take a sword in your hands is your intention to cut the enemy, whatever the means. Whenever you parry, hit, spring, strike or touch the enemy's cutting sword, you must cut the enemy in the same movement. It is essential to attain this. If you think only of hitting, springing, striking or touching the enemy, you will not be able actually to cut him.

- Miyamoto Musashi

My Experience

"It's what Jason Bourne uses," remarks my brother. I was spacing out before, so I don't know what the hell he's talking about. But now I'm hooked – if I have one man-crush, it's Jason Bourne. Talk about a real badass.

"What does he use?!" I demand to know.

"Krav Maga," replies my bro, "it's the martial art he uses to obliterate all of those poor dudes in the movies."

My mouth drops open and visions of me demolishing a horde of bros fill my mind. *I'm doing it.*

Krav Maga is a self-defense system developed for use by the Israeli Defense Forces, and its basic principle is ending a fight or encounter as quickly and brutally as possible. Knees to the groin and elbows to the face are common fare. That's also why it's not practiced competitively like MMA or boxing.

It turns out Jason Bourne doesn't actually use Krav Maga, but after reading up on it I was sold. I signed up at an academy that was located on the way back home from work, so I'd be more inclined to show up for class on a consistent basis.

I clearly recall my first day. After a quick talk from the head master, I headed out to the mats and joined a crew of dudes stretching in preparation for class. Keep in mind I've always thought of myself as supremely athletic and fit – so much so that I chose to come to class on a night that I had a basketball game directly afterwards. "I wouldn't recommend it," one of the instructors told me on the phone, "it can be pretty intense." But his words fell on deaf ears.

We started with some jogging, pushups, and burpees – nothing crazy, but I was a bit tired after the warm up. Then we moved onto the *technique* portion of class. It was punch defense. I matched up with a slender, tall Russian guy. We were instructed to throw punches, half-speed, at each other. The defendant was to make a defense and then follow up with a few combatives (punches, knees, elbows, etc.).

I took my turn on defense and repeated the basic defense the instructor demonstrated, meeting him wrist to wrist to deflect the punch, and then throwing a few punches over his shoulder, to mimic a real life counter attack. And then it was his turn...

Without much of a thought I threw a punch with my right hand. Next thing you know, I'm on my ass. My whole body is in pain, and I'm feeling a bit dizzy. The dude deflected my punch, bent me over, threw a couple light knees into my chest, and then placed his palm underneath my chin to throw me back onto my butt. "Take it easy on him," the instructor said.

God, I feel like a little bitch.

I wish I could say that was the worst of it. But after that drill, we moved onto the *endurance* portion of class. Today that meant having one guy hold you back with a rope looped around your waist, while you fought to advance forward against the resistance and throw punches at another guy – holding a punching bag in front of you. Sweet Jesus this was terrible. By the time I'd fought my way forward to the bag, I was already gassed. As soon as I stopped to throw a punch, the dude from behind yanked me back across the room. Talk about 100 percent effort.

After one time through this drill, I was ready to vomit, go home, and sleep. But we continued – for a lot longer. By the time class was over, I'd been put into my place. I was humbled, bruised, and exhausted. Needless to say, I wasn't the MVP of the ball game that night. I was barely a participant.

Rule 5: Learn to Fight

Every man should be able to defend himself physically. If you live in a first world country today, this is not something you will need to rely on consistently, but nonetheless it's a necessary part of becoming an alpha male. Furthermore, a certain confidence comes with knowing how to fight. Fear disappears from the trained fighter's mind. He knows he can defend himself when the shit hits the fan, and this manifests itself through increased confidence in all social situations.

Take Action

1. Research the characteristics of different martial arts (Krav Maga, Brazilian Ju-Jitsu, Muay Thai, etc.).
2. Pick one that's appealing to you.
3. Find a school or academy that offers classes nearby.
4. Sign up and start going to class.

Chapter 6
How to be self-reliant

All life is an experiment. The more experiments you make the better.

- Ralph Waldo Emerson

My Experience

My stomach sucks.

Literally, I can't even begin to name all of the little things that set it off. If I eat something with lactose, boom! I'll be farting all day. If I eat late at night, boom! I'll be pooping all morning. If I eat too early in the morning, boom! More poop and farts than you can handle.

This condition, or series of conditions, has led me to try all different types of diets. Well, it eventually did. All through college I sort of just dealt with the consequences. But recently I've tried everything from dairy free and gluten free to intermittent fasting.

Eating dairy free helped a lot. Most of the bloating and farts went away, but I'd still have them in the morning. That's where intermittent fasting came in. For some reason if I don't eat late at night, or early in the morning, I'm able to avoid the morning discomforts. I'm not sure why. This isn't even one of the benefits that people who intermittently fast report. Well, I'm reporting it right now.

So now I avoid dairy and intermittently fast. I no longer pass gas like Steve Nash drops dimes on the basketball court. And my stomach feels great almost all of the time. I still indulge from time to time, eating pizza or ice cream, and then I pay the price. But for the most part, my stomach puzzle is solved – all because I conducted a series of experiments on my body.

Rule 6: Experiment More

While most people rely on others for feedback and information, the alpha takes this outside information into account, but he relies primarily on his own experience – his own experiments.

If it wasn't for experimenting, I would not have done many of the things I have – from gaming girls and learning how to fight to putting on muscle and changing careers. Other people's wisdom can only take you so far. You must try new things yourself to uncover the only truth that matters – how a particular thing vibes, affects, and meshes with you – with your body, with your mind.

Take Action

1. Next time you find yourself thinking, *does X or Y really work?* – catch yourself and recognize it.
2. Rather than Googling the topic at hand, go do it. Try it out.

Try one of the following examples right now: Wake up early tomorrow, meditate, try to freestyle rap, turn on a song and dance, do squats at the gym, approach five cute girls at the mall, introduce yourself to five women on an online dating site, intermittently fast (eat only from 12PM to 8PM), try a yoga class, don't fap for the next week, or start a daily journal.

Chapter 7

A simple trick to revolutionize your productivity

It is always your next move.

- Napoleon Hill

My Experience

I decided I wanted to get my personal training certification. At this point, I had no intention of leaving my job or changing careers.

My cousin had recently begun working as a personal trainer. We had been longtime workout buddies, and my competitive side didn't want to fall far behind him, in terms of exercise science knowledge. So I made it my mission to get certified.

Two months passed and I had made no headway. At the time I was reading *Getting Things Done* by David Allen. The whole book revolves around the premise that productivity's main enemy is inaction – things tend to get put off and ignored if immediate action isn't taken. The main remedy offered in the book is determining a series of next actions you must take for any particular project.

While reading this, it hit me that I'd done absolutely nothing since deciding to get certified. It wasn't because I was being lazy, or didn't really want to take the time to do it. Well, maybe I was being lazy, but I did really want the certification. So I laid out a series of actions I would have to take in order to achieve my goal, from taking the actual test all the way backwards to just getting on Amazon and ordering the damn textbook.

The result was powerful. I cruised through buying the book, studying the material on a daily basis, paying for the test, taking practice tests, scheduling a test date, and finally taking and passing it – all in a couple of months. To put that in perspective, I know people who've signed up for 6 month courses on the studying portion alone. This was efficiency at its finest, my friends.

Rule 7: Know Your Next Move

Alpha males are organized. They take action. They don't sit back and hope for things to happen. For every mission you choose to take on in life, you must always know the very next action that needs to be taken. Otherwise, you will stall out completely or fail to achieve the mission in a timely manner.

Take Action

Now you see why I've included this section in every chapter, and done so with step-by-step lists.

1. Pick one of your current missions.
2. Explicitly define the outcome necessary to declare the mission accomplished.
3. Working backwards, define every step that must be taken to get there.
4. Complete the first step.

Example: I will write and publish an eBook. By February 1st it will be live on the Amazon.com bookstore for Kindle.

Steps required to get there: submit the book's html file to Amazon.com, submit the book's description and pricing to Amazon.com, send out review copies of the book to 15 bloggers, format the word document appropriately and save it as an html file, have a copywriter edit the book, review and edit the book, write the book, outline the book, choose a topic for the book.

I find that *Wunderlist,* an application for smartphones and computers, does a great job at tracking your next actions. Its functionality is simple – it's a list of checklists. In my case, I create a list for each mission, and then add the next actions as checklist items.

Link: https://www.wunderlist.com

Additionally, I suggest reading *Getting Things Done* by David Allen for a more in depth look at specific systems that can be used for doing this more efficiently.

Chapter 8

How to make time for your passions

Action expresses priorities.

- Mahatma Gandhi

My Experience

I decided to write a book.

When it comes to fitness, the amount of bullshit on the internet is overwhelming. Everyone is trying to sell you a magic pill when the only true quick fix that exists is anabolic steroids – and everybody shuns those. But people don't want to hear this. They want to believe there is a cheap, harmless magic pill that will do the work for them.

I spent countless days, weeks, and months trying different approaches and finally found it's the least glamorous of approaches that work the best. I've always been a smaller dude, so I wanted to build muscle. After two years of counting calories to ensure steady weight gain, and pushing myself in the gym to get stronger, I'd put on around 35 pounds, and most of it was muscle. I'd also gone through periods of losing weight to cut fat, and done so successfully.

I'd solved the puzzle, and I wanted to share how simple training and nutrition really are – and use scientific studies and research to back it all up. I just wanted to simplify the basics that most people are completely unaware of. So I went through the exercise of defining all the next actions I needed to write and publish a book that would do exactly that.

Damn it, I don't have time for this, I thought. Every weekday after work I either hit the gym or went to an hour-long Krav Maga class. By the time I got home all I wanted to do was eat dinner and sleep. And I was studying for my certification – so I put the book off.

Then one night I was eating dinner – two juicy burgers fresh off my George Foreman grill. After I terminated the patties, I finished watching the episode of Breaking Bad I'd put on to accompany my feast. Then it hit me – *I could be writing my book right now*. But I was thoroughly exhausted. I just wanted to turn my brain off and chill for an hour or so before hitting the sack.

Then it hit me again. This isn't a weekday only activity. I'd been cruising through episodes of Breaking Bad like an addict, even on the weekends. "What else am I doing on the weekends?" I thought. *Lifting, reading, and going out.* Not bad, but I realized there was still more than enough time to commit at least one hour a day to researching and writing the book.

Within a matter of months I'd completed my first book – *The Simple Art of Bodybuilding: A Practical Guide to Training and Nutrition.* After a good deal of promotion it became an Amazon best seller. I get monthly royalty payouts from Amazon to this day. And it all came together because I dedicated a few hours each weekend to writing, instead of shooting the shit.

Rule 8: Find Time to Achieve

If you don't have time for something, it's not a priority. No, you don't have to be a productivity machine who works every hour of every day. But be honest with yourself – do you REALLY have no time to do x, y, and z? I found time to get certified as a personal trainer, write a book, start a blog, lift, learn Krav Maga, game two nights a week, and read a whole bunch of books while working my 9-5. And I still spent time watching TV, playing video games, and going out at night.

Take Action

1. List every mission you currently want to accomplish
2. List all of the next-actions necessary for accomplishing each mission (if you haven't yet).
3. Schedule time in your week when you can tackle some of these actions – even if only for 30 minutes. In fact, I find that committing to just 30 minutes is a great strategy for making yourself do something.

Chapter 9
How to overcome the fear of failure

Far better is it to dare mighty things, to win glorious triumphs, even though checkered by failure... than to rank with those poor spirits who neither enjoy nor suffer much, because they live in a gray twilight that knows not victory nor defeat.

- Theodore Roosevelt

My Experience

It was a humid summer Saturday night in Boston.

I was reading an eBook about approach anxiety, and it suggested logging on to an online pickup artist community to look for a wingman in my area. I was bored, so I entertained the idea for a moment. I had no real intention of actually following through – it seemed creepy. But going out with my friends always turned into a drunken mess, with few or no actual approaches made. So I figured *what the hell.*

I went to the website and it turns out there was a guy looking for a wingman in Boston that very night. I hesitantly sent him a private message, still not taking the whole thing seriously. Before you know it I was dressed in some *going-out* clothes, and driving down to meet him at the Boston Commons. I was nervous, I won't lie. And I had a backup plan, I swear. If he turned out to be a creepy old man or something weird like that, I was going to meet up with my real friends at a bar nearby.

I arrived and met Evan and Jack. Evan was a recent graduate who was brand new to the pickup community, same as me. We immediately hit it off. Jack, on the other hand, was a bit older and a little on the creepy side. However, he told us he'd been doing this for a while, and seemed confident in his skills. Our relative comfort with each other outweighed the obscurity of his character.

As soon as we entered the bar, he was off. He had talked to three girls and kissed at least one before Evan and I had even made a single approach. "Ok," I said, finally taking the lead, "let's go talk to those two girls in the corner." Evan nodded, and followed me over.

"Hey guys, quick question – which one of you has the most money?" I asked, reciting a silly opener (pickup lingo for pickup line or opening phrase).

"Ummmm, that's an odd question. I guess Jessica does," she said, motioning towards her friend.

"Cool, I'm sick of working so I'm out looking for a sugar momma," I replied.

"Excuse me?" the first girl said. I had mumbled the punch line, she hadn't heard it, and I lost all confidence. We walked away.

And that was the worst of it. That opener sucks, and actually became something we often said at the beginning of a night to get rejection out of the way. After facing the fear of failure once, we'd loosen up and crush it the rest of the night.

By the time that first night had ended, we'd approached four or five more sets of girls. We didn't get any numbers or make-outs, but we were hooked. The thrill of the approach was exciting. We were nervous every time.

That's what kept us coming back for more. Evan and I remain close friends to this day. We went out two nights a week religiously for the next year. We both improved our game drastically, approached hundreds, if not thousands of girls, got plenty of numbers, dates, kisses, and more. Jack, on the other hand, got black-out drunk that night. I had to put him in a cab home – literally.

Rule 9: Get Rejected

Alpha males aren't fearless; rather they accept the presence of a fear and then face it anyway. They don't let it paralyze them, or stop them in their tracks. They know that failure is an inevitable part of life, but they push on anyway.

The girls and sex that came with practicing game in such a dedicated manner were awesome. But the greater benefit I derived from my experiences was developing the habit of leaving my comfort zone. In game, you must approach continually – in spite of probable rejection. A normal night out would consist of around 20 approaches, and most were rejections – whether that meant right away, while asking for a number, going for a kiss, or when trying to leave the venue. I had to acknowledge the fear of failure every night I went out, and then push through anyway. It was a rejection therapy of sorts.

If it wasn't for game, I wonder whether or not I would've had the balls to quit my job and take the risk of changing careers from software to writing and personal training, where good money is far from guaranteed.

Take Action

Following the steps below may be the single most important and powerful thing you can do to initiate rapid momentum in your life. Fear, in particular the fear of failure, is what holds us back from attempting greatness on a daily basis. By practicing getting rejected you'll quickly familiarize yourself with the process of failing, and this will develop a powerful resistance to fear in your character. Your inhibitions to attempt, and eventually accomplish, ambitious missions will be forever lowered.

1. Ask 10 attractive girls where the closest coffee shop is, and follow up by telling them that they're looking good today.
2. Tell 10 attractive girls that they're cute, and you had to say hi.
3. Ask 10 attractive girls for their number, so you can hang out soon.

I find that approaching girls is a universal fear among men, even those who've practiced pickup for a long time. This is because the fear of failure is so prevalent. That's why I recommend it for rejection therapy. Also, check out the link below for one guy's experiment of getting rejected 100 different ways.

Link: http://www.fearbuster.com/100-days-of-rejection-therapy

Chapter 10

An essential quality of every leader

The price of greatness is responsibility.

- Winston Churchill

My Experience

It's a regular Tuesday in the office.

Last week my team put together the final touches on the largest project that we'd completed since I've been here. The solution we put in place went live on the client's servers yesterday – so far, so good.

"Motherfucker," I hear my boss mumble under his breath. His cubicle is adjacent to mine. I patiently wait for what comes next.

He slowly gets out of his seat, and walks over. The four members of our team all sit in close proximity. "Guys, someone screwed up," he begins his rant. I won't go into details of what went wrong, because it might take up half of my book to explain properly. But he went on for more than a couple of minutes. In short, I was working on a system that output the data needed by one of my colleagues, and a system he set up. His system output the final product, which was completely FUBAR (nerd-talk for Fucked Up Beyond All Recognition).

I wasn't sure what went wrong – it could have been more than a thousand different things. But I knew there was a decent chance it was on my end. "That's my bad," I proclaimed. In an instant, my boss's tone changed. The last thing he expected was for the youngest, most inexperienced member of the team to step up and take the blame. He was shocked, I believe.

I was still listening to Brian Tracy's *The Luck Factor* at the time. That morning, I listened to the chapter on taking responsibility, and it obviously struck a chord.

My colleagues' reactions cemented this new principle into my life. While I was reprimanded to a small degree, I began to notice I was getting far more respect from the senior members of the team. Since then, I try to take every chance I can to take responsibility for my actions, both in and outside of work. It's very empowering.

Rule 10: Take Full Responsibility

When you take full responsibility for everything you do in life, both internal and external, it creates an extremely powerful effect. On one hand, you feel in control and stop blaming others for every little problem. On the other hand, others will respect you and begin to look to you as a leader. These are both essential qualities of the alpha male.

Take Action

1. Commit to taking responsibility for everything in life. Tell yourself right now: "I am fully responsible for everything that happens to me and has happened to me."
2. The next time you feel the impulse to blame someone else for something: stop, take a deep breath, and take the blame –

even if you don't fully deserve it.

3. The next time someone comes your way, looking for a culprit, take the blame – even if you had almost no hand in the event in question. If you had absolutely zero involvement, then don't take the blame – that would be dishonest.

Chapter 11
Why lying will destroy your life

Honesty is the first chapter in the book of wisdom.

- Thomas Jefferson

My Experience

I'd finally finished my book, *The Simple Art of Bodybuilding*. It was nearly perfect, I thought.

Before I published it, I wanted to let a few others look over it. That way I could make a few small tweaks, here or there, to polish it off.

I sent it out to a few close friends, family members, and one Sebastian Marshall. Yes, the same Sebastian Marshall who wrote *Ikigai,* the book that changed my life. I'd reached out to him a few months earlier when I was starting a blog, without much hope for a response. His blog was inspirational (http://www.sebastianmarshall.com), and I wanted to bounce a few ideas off of him. He was extremely helpful then, so I hoped he would respond again.

Not only did he respond, but he sent me multiple pages of in-depth analysis about my book. In short, and in far kinder words, he said it sucked and wasn't ready. It wasn't all negative, as he acknowledged that the base of something valuable had been laid, but nonetheless, I was crushed. He suggested a few possible routes I could take to create a superior product.

After all the work I had done over the past few months, I had no desire to do anything other than publish it. If someone else had told me the same, I would've told them to *fuck off* and published it anyway. But Sebastian was a mentor to me, someone I held in high regard.

After re-reading my own book I realized he was right. While there was a lot of good info, it lacked anything that would set it apart from the myriad of other fitness books available. I'd been looking at my own book through rose-colored glasses. I viewed an average work as a masterpiece, all because it was my creation.

I took his advice to heart and got back to work. I began by adding more in-depth explanations and examples throughout the book. Next, I scoured the web and science journals for scientific studies that would back up all of my claims. This part was eye-opening. While most of my beliefs were verified, others had no real backing, and I was forced to change.

After editing the book to incorporate Sebastian's advice, the result was nothing short of spectacular. The book regularly sits atop the Amazon.com best seller list for Men's Health, has brought hundreds of new subscribers to my blog, and provided an ample audience for my second book. I have no doubt that if I hadn't come to terms with reality and taken an honest look at the book, it would never have sold well – or even at all.

Rule 11: Be Brutally Honest

Being honest with others is one thing, but being honest with yourself is a whole different ballgame – one that most men fail at. Both are equally important. When you lie to another person you violate their trust, and display weakness. You cave into the fear of what others will think of you for expressing the truth. When you lie to yourself, you misrepresent something in your mind, and when your perception of the world doesn't match up with reality, the chance of success diminishes greatly. Alpha males don't lie, to themselves or to others.

My book is one example of this – had I not been honest with myself and come to terms with reality, it would've never done well. Another would be if I hadn't faced the reality that I wasn't going to get laid if I didn't approach women and work at improving my game. Many men refuse to accept the truth that they aren't great with women, and they never get any better. I was in this same boat for years, and I never made any real progress as a result.

Take Action

1. Admit any past lies you can think of – to yourself, friends, co-workers and family. Call someone right now and confess a past lie, no matter how small or distant.
2. Going forward, practice radical honesty on simple things like whether or not you farted, ate the last donut, or don't like someone's idea.
3. Practice tact – just because a girl is ugly or you feel like shit doesn't mean you need to proclaim it to everyone in the room. Choose to say nothing when it's better than speaking the truth.

Chapter 12

How to fix your posture

What you do speaks so loud that I cannot hear what you say.

- Ralph Waldo Emerson

My Experience

My roommate Craig and I are on the way to meet another friend of mine, Nick, for a beer. They are both close friends of mine, but have never met each other.

We arrive at the bar and Nick's already there, seated and waiting for us. "What's up," he says, greeting us in a deep voice, and offering a firm handshake at the same time. A few rounds of drinks later, we call it a night. On the way out I notice Craig staring at Nick with a confused look on his face. I'm curious, but don't mention anything at the time.

The next day I find out why. After a day's work I'm preparing dinner in the kitchen, sautéing some vegetables in olive oil on the frying pan. "I couldn't believe how short your friend was," Craig exclaims as he enters the room. Nick comes in at a whopping five feet and three inches – on a good day.

"Yeah, he's tiny. Was that why you were eyeing him once we finally stood up?" I reply.

"Dude, exactly. I couldn't believe it. But he has quite the presence." I've known Nick for years and never paid much attention to it, but it's true – I don't look at him the same way I look at other guys who are that short. "I would've guessed he was taller than me before we all stood up," Craig continues.

Since then, Craig and I continue to joke about this phenomenon to this day. Every time Nick comes up in conversation one of us is quick to call him by his new nickname, *The Presence*.

Rule 12: Stand Tall

I learned an important lesson from *The Presence*. If a guy that short can pull off a dominant appearance, I should be able to take it to the next level and have people straight up trembling in their shoes. Well, that might not be so good, but you get the point.

Having good posture and standing up straight goes a long way. People perceive you as confident and strong, regardless of how you're feeling or what you're saying. Furthermore, studies have shown that by practicing strong body language you actually begin to feel more confident. The body reflects how you're feeling and how you're feeling is also a reflection of how you're holding your body. Needless to say, an alpha male always stands tall and displays a confident, strong posture.

Take Action

1. Hold the crown of your head high. To practice this: stand up, press your upper back and butt against a wall behind you, tuck your chin down towards your chest, and then tilt your head back until it touches the wall. This will give you an idea of how you should be holding your head.

2. Pull your shoulder blades back, as not to slouch. Imagine that you're trying to squeeze a nickel in between your shoulder blades. One way to correct this over time, if you're a chronic sloucher, is to stretch your chest by grabbing both sides of a door-frame with your hands and then leaning forward through it.

3. Move with a slow and deliberate pace. Constant fidgeting wastes energy and signals nervousness.

Also, check out the following info-graphic – *The Ultimate Guide to Good Posture* by greatest.com – it's pretty cool.

Link: http://greatist.com/health/ultimate-guide-good-posture-work-infographic

Chapter 13

How to always be confident

If I loved myself truly and deeply, would I let myself experience this?

- Kamal Ravikant

My Experience

Tonight is my third summer league basketball game.

We won the first game and lost the second. My play had been sporadic. It always has been, really. All the way from high school and AAU basketball through college I'd been a head case on the court. Sometimes I had all the confidence in the world and my handles were tight, my three pointers were wet, and I could finish with ease. Other times, I was so unsure of myself that my hands would literally shake, and I could barely catch a pass or string together a few dribbles.

At the time I was reading *Love Yourself Like Your Life Depends On It* By Kamal Ravikant. The whole premise of the book is that we often forget to love ourselves, and remind ourselves that we do – and it leads to loads of unnecessary suffering. It might be the most touching and important book I've ever read.

The game is about to start. I lace up my kicks tightly, slowly walk to center court, and shake hands with a couple players on the other team. We line up around the center circle, the whistle blows, and the ref tosses the opening tip up into the air.

The first possession our best shooter Mitch bangs home a three. "Buckets!" I yell, trying to boost his confidence. Next their best player, a 6'2" black kid with a strong build (I'm not racist – this is basketball we're talking about, and I'm a 5'10" white boy), dribbles the ball up court. I'm covering him. I always cover the opposition's best guard. We make eye contact, and hold it for three or four seconds. *It's on.* He comes at me hard to the right then gives a hesitation crossover to the left, passing me in the process and laying it in. *Fuck.*

I take the inbound pass, ready for redemption. As I cross half court, the same player, now defending me, comes up to play tight, aggressive defense. I hesitate. He swipes, and takes the ball from me. "I'll take that," he says, taunting me. Before I know it he's laid it in for another two points.

The negative mental chatter begins to kick in. *Not this again. I fucking suck tonight.* I'm down on myself and want the game to be over, just two minutes in. Then it hits me, and I hear Kamal's voice in the back of my head:

If I loved myself truly and deeply, would I let myself experience this?

Hell no, I fucking love myself. I love myself. I love myself. I began to repeat this in my head and under my breath. "I'm in control of my thoughts, I love myself, and I'm going to crush it tonight."

When I shift my focus back to the game, we're on defense, and the other team just put up a deep shot. I body my man – hard – and then sky for the rebound. After coming down with the ball I immediately push up court. I'm dribbling up the right sideline, with my man pressing me on my left side. I hold him off with a combination of my left shoulder and forearm. As we approach the basket, the bumping and jockeying for position intensifies. But I'm determined. I pick up my dribble, give him one last bump, and lay it in with a finger roll off my right hand.

"That's all day!" I yell, looking deep into his eyes. He's pissed, but I love it.

The rest of that season I played with supreme confidence.

Rule 13: Love Yourself

You must love yourself – like your life depends on it. This is the single most important lesson I've learned in my life. Almost everyone gets so caught up in worrying and stressing about silly little things that they forget to love themselves. Often, people even grow to hate themselves. This is unacceptable. You won't enjoy life, build quality relationships, accomplish big goals, and become alpha until you fully and wholly accept yourself exactly as you are now. Not just accept, but deeply love.

You must care for yourself with the same affection as you would with a close loved one. I'm not saying to brag and be an egotistical dick, only that you must love yourself as you are. It's impossible to put the powerful effects of loving yourself into words – it's something you have to do on your own.

Take Action

I've borrowed some of the following advice from Kamal's book, which I highly suggest you read for yourself.

1. Right now, and every morning going forward, look yourself in the mirror and say "I love myself" 10 times.
2. Think about the most recent time you began to doubt or get down on yourself. Ask yourself "If I loved myself truly and deeply, would I have let myself experience this?"
3. Answer the question, and use this technique in similar situations going forward.
4. Say "I love myself" again. Do it often.

Chapter 14

A simple way to remove stress and increase focus

Meditation is the dissolution of thoughts in eternal awareness or pure consciousness without objectification, knowing without thinking, merging finitude in infinity.

- Voltaire

My Experience

I close my eyes.

This is pointless, I think.

"This is pointless," I say. My brother reassures me to be patient, "You have to give it a chance, just focus on your breath for the next five minutes."

"Ugh, okay." *Breathe in, breathe out, breathe in* - oh man, I feel my tummy grumbling. *I'm fucking starving.* An image of a juicy double cheeseburger with crispy bacon on top enters my mind. "Dude, all I can think about is cheeseburgers," I whisper, half-respecting the silence my brother seeks.

"You don't get it. When your mind wanders it's okay, just recognize it, and return to the breath – it won't be easy," he responds.

"Yes, sensei." I close my eyes and return my focus to the breathing.

Breathe in, breathe out, breathe in, breathe out, brea... damn I hope that one girl I met over the weekend texts me back. And I catch myself. *Not now, David - breathe in, breathe out, breathe in...*

About five minutes and twenty mental interruptions later, we're done. At least I am. "I actually feel pretty good," I remark. "Like relaxed, but focused."

Rule 14: Meditate

Meditation is amazing because it offers relief from everything else you're doing during the day – all of the worrying, talking, thinking, achieving, confronting, lifting, reading, writing, driving, banging – everything. It's an opportunity to turn your mind off and rest. No regrets from the past, no worries about the future.

But it's not that simple. Turning your mind off is hard. If there was an on/off switch somewhere, I would've turned that bitch off a long time ago. What I've learned is that turning your mind off is the goal, not a participation requirement. I view meditation as practice for turning off my brain.

When I've been good about meditating, I do far better, and enjoy consecutive minutes of emptiness – vacation from the constant bombardment of shit we face every minute of every day, both good and bad. I return feeling fresh, and ready to fuck shit up – whether that means writing this book, lifting heavy weights, or talking to girls.

All alpha males should possess this key skill, because otherwise it's all too easy to get caught up in pettiness and unproductive thoughts or thought patterns.

Take Action

If you have access to the internet, then try out a guided meditation on YouTube – the one below is my favorite.

Link: http://www.youtube.com/watch?v=QcD9bdu6xdM

Otherwise, use the guidelines below.

1. Find a comfortable posture. I prefer to lay on my back, but many people enjoy simply sitting.
2. Close your eyes.
3. Focus on your breaths for the next five minutes. Inhale through your nose and deep in your stomach, and then exhale fully.

Practice meditation once a day.

Chapter 15

How to always be in control of your thoughts

Feelings come and go like clouds in a windy sky. Conscious breathing is my anchor.

- Thich Nhat Hanh

My Experience

I had just finished conducting an interview with JC Deen (www.JCDFitness.com) for my fitness blog (www.BornToBulk.com). Afterwards, he suggested I check out Elliot Hulse's YouTube channel. "He's a friend," he said. "He's got a lot of good content on lifting, but also just on life in general."

So I open up Google Chrome, go to YouTube, and search for *Elliot Hulse*. He has two channels. One is called *Strength Camp* and is about weight lifting, and the other is called *Elliot Hulse* and its subtitle is *Ideas for Living Stronger*.

I've had enough fitness talk for the day so I click on the second channel (http://www.youtube.com/user/elliottsaidwhat). *Holy shit!* This dude has hundreds of thousands of subscribers. I'm intrigued to say the least. I click on one of his *popular* videos – *How to create a deeper voice*. I remember his large, masculine face coming onto the screen. I remember his deep voice, "Often I talk about breathing into your balls. Well, before [when I had a high pitched voice] I was breathing in a castrated fashion."

I look at the clock. An hour has passed – maybe two. All I know is that I've watched a lot of this guy's videos, and he's fucking awesome. *It's true,* I thought. *He does talk about breathing into your balls a lot.* And in regards to a lot more things than just speaking with a deep voice. If his confident and poised presence is any indicator, he's definitely onto something.

Two days later. I'm at a college bar with my buddy Evan. "Those two," he says, pointing to two cute girls seated at a table in the corner. He wants me to approach them, of course.

"Ok, one sec." I haven't spoken to any girls yet, and I'm nervous.

He encourages me, "Don't be a pussy, c'mon let's go." Tough love is our style.

I feel my heart pounding. My chest tightens. And my breaths are shallow and quick.

And my breaths are shallow and quick.

Oh shit! I think to myself. *Elliot, I will make you proud.* I take a long and deep breath, into my stomach and eventually my balls. And then another – and another. My heart rate slows, my body loosens up, and the haze of negativity leaves my mind.

Ok, let's do this. I set my eyes on my target. "The blonde one is mine, follow me." Evan smiles, and we're off.

Rule 15: Breathe Deeply

Conscious breathing is possibly an alpha male's number one tool. It calms the nerves and controls your mental state.

If your breaths are quick and shallow, only reaching the back of your throat or upper chest, you'll feel nervous or anxious. If your breaths are full and deep, reaching down into your belly and your balls, you'll feel like the calm and confident man that you're meant to be.

Meditation has become breathing practice for me – that's literally how I think about it. When I meditate, I focus all of my attention on my breathing. I feel the cool air come in through my nose and slowly work its way down into my belly, finishing in my balls. Then I exhale and feel the air come back up my spine and leave through my nose – this time accompanied by a warm sensation.

This experience both invigorates and relaxes my entire body. I try to practice this type of breathing when I'm meditating and throughout the day, especially when I'm feeling particularly anxious or flustered.

Take Action

Right now, take a few breaths, as described below.

1. Inhale through your nose, and feel the air fill your chest – then exhale fully. Do it four more times.
2. Inhale through your nose, and feel the air move into your upper abdomen – then exhale fully. Do it four more times.
3. Inhale a third time, and feel the air move deeper into your lower belly and your balls – then exhale slowly and fully. Do it four more times.

How did you feel as you completed each series of breaths? Do it again.

Next time you catch yourself in a bad mood or high pressure situation, stop. Take a few deep breaths into your balls, and focus on the process as you go. You'll immediately feel a calming relief, a feeling of control.

Chapter 16
Why this one activity will ruin your life

There is no dignity when the human dimension is eliminated from the person. In short, the problem with pornography is not that it shows too much of the person, but that it shows far too little.

- Pope John Paul II

My Experience

4 AM on a Wednesday night.

I wake up, and feel the urge to pee. *Ugh, I hate this.* It's one of those situations where I just want to go back to sleep, but I know I'm going to wake up again in 30 minutes for the same reason.

Fuck it. I slowly and reluctantly get out of bed and stumble to the bathroom, only half awake. I've made a habit of just getting up and doing it. It usually works well, and I fall right back to sleep. But there are dangers. And no, one of those dangers is not masturbation – stop thinking ahead.

As I come back into my room, I see the blue LED light on my phone flashing. Here's one danger. *Hmmm, I wonder who emailed me.* I click my phone, type in the pass code, and swipe down on the notification bar. It's a YouTube email with new videos from my favorite channels. The top one is from the Ted Talks channel – it's a video about pornography.

I don't know why I didn't lock my phone and go back to sleep, but I'm rarely rational at 4 AM on a weeknight, or any night, for that matter. I click the link and proceed to watch a 20 minute video about porn, and its negative effects on the mind and the body – *very interesting.*

I won't go into personal details and revelations, because frankly I'm not comfortable telling the world about that. I'm trying my best to be completely transparent and open in writing this book, but I must draw the line somewhere. This is where.

Rule 16: Stop Watching Porn

No scientific studies have been conclusive in analyzing porn's effects on men. This is because literally every dude starts jerking it to porn when he's like 14 years old. There's no control group – an essential part of any experiment.

But there have been growing movements of young adults abstaining from porn, especially in large online communities like reddit and the bodybuilding.com forums. They call it *no fap,* and preach the various benefits they've received from quitting porn. These benefits range from decreased social anxiety and erectile dysfunction relief to a newfound motivation to search out a real life sexual partner.

The truth is that the act of masturbating to porn is so different than real sex. You're watching other people do it – on a screen. Do you think that's alpha?

Some scientists have theorized that this causes your brain to be re-wired and associate sexual arousal and pleasure with patterns of pixels on a computer screen, rather than a real female's touch. Furthermore, this arousal becomes increasingly more complex, as you must flip between tabs and different girls in order to maintain interest.

In short, it's a recipe for disaster.

Take Action

1. Stop watching porn. That's it.
2. Next time you have the urge, remind yourself (a) that you're putting off finding a real partner, (b) that you're potentially re-wiring your brain in a dangerous manner, and (c) that you run the risk of developing a number of miserable side-effects. There is no positive. Give it up.
3. If you still have the urge – meditate for five minutes. I guarantee you that the urge will have dissipated by the time you're done.

Here's the Ted Talk video I mentioned:

Link: http://www.youtube.com/watch?v=wSF82AwSDiU

Also, check out this cool info-graphic on porn and *no fap:*

Link: http://i.huffpost.com/gen/1377666/original.jpg

Chapter 17
How to get the most out of both success and failure

There are three methods to gaining wisdom. The first is reflection, which is the highest.

- Confucius

My Experience

Monday morning.

It feels like any other day. The weekend was fun and relaxing, but nothing crazy happened – for the better or for the worse. But something is very different on this particular Monday.

I've chosen to adopt a new habit. Every morning I will do a review of the previous day. I forget where I encountered this suggestion, but wherever it was compelled me to give it a try. Here I go.

What did I do well this weekend?

Let's see. I banged out a few sections of the National Academy of Sports Medicine book I'm studying to become certified as a personal trainer. This is an increase in productivity from most weekends. Also, Saturday night I went out and got three numbers at the bar. They were all from cute girls I legitimately enjoyed talking with. I plan on texting all three. Not a personal record, but great work nonetheless.

What would I do differently?

Hmmm. I would advance my interactions with those three girls next time, and attempt a kiss. It's great that I got their numbers, but I need to continue to push myself farther outside my comfort zone.

Rule 17: Reflect

While that particular weekend seemed completely insignificant to me on Monday morning, the action of reflecting on it gave it meaning. Time that otherwise would've been forgotten, now had a particular context and significance attached to it.

I know it wasn't a particular news-worthy weekend, but that's why I chose to write about it. When something relatively large happens in your life (new job, new girlfriend, being fired, losing a friend, etc.) you tend to consciously acknowledge and meditate on it. However, when it seems like just another day, you tend to forget it and label it as ordinary or commonplace in your memory. This is dangerous, because there's a good chance you're glossing over important events that you could learn large life lessons from.

The alpha male is ever self-aware, so that he can consciously make informed decisions and changes to his life – rather than floating aimlessly through it. By reflecting daily, you accomplish exactly this.

Take Action

Right now, and every morning going forward, ask yourself and answer the following two questions. Doing so on paper is far better, but even doing so in your head can be valuable.

1. What did I do well yesterday?
2. What will I do differently, next time a similar situation occurs?

Chapter 18
How to instantly boost your charisma

You can make more friends in two months by becoming interested in other people than you can in two years by trying to get other people interested in you.

- Dale Carnegie

My Experience

Saturday afternoon.

My friend John is visiting from New York. We lived together senior year of college. "Hey do you mind if Mack and Josh swing by?" he asks me. Mack and Josh lived on the floor below us when we were in school. They were both really friendly dudes, but John was far better friends with them than I was and therefore I hadn't seen them since graduation.

"Of course not, invite them over."

An hour passes, and they arrive. After the initial greetings and pleasantries are over, we sit down. "What the hell have you been up to?" Mack asks me.

"I'm working for a software company right now, but I'm also in the process of getting my personal training certification," I respond.

"Dude, that's awesome! Are you thinking about changing careers?"

I think for a moment, then answer, "I'm not sure, I'm hesitant to do so because of how highly regarded my current job is in relation to personal training."

"But what do you really want to do?" he follows up.

"If money weren't an issue, I'd definitely choose to train." Our conversation continues for a long time, an hour maybe. Over the course of the talk, he continually asks me questions about my interest in fitness, and the crossroads I'm approaching in life.

Since that day, I consider Mack to be one of my closest friends. We stay in touch, and constantly advise each other on everything from girls and fitness to careers and life.

Rule 18: Take an Interest in Others

Mack became nearly my best friend after one hour of talking to me. This is remarkable. He did it all by doing just one simple thing – talking to me and asking me about things that I have a deep interest in, namely my life and fitness. That's all it takes.

Everyone loves to talk about themselves, and their main interests and hobbies, whether that means fitness, travel, poker, sports, stocks, movies, books, etc. As an alpha male, you should be able to tap into this conversational power and quickly begin building rapport, influence, and respect in others.

Take Action

Call up a friend right now and do the following. Also do the same with all friends, family, and strangers going forward.

1. Focus your conversation on the other person.
2. Ask them about what they're up to.
3. Based on their response, dig deeper and ask questions about things they're interested in or activities they're involved in.

For a deeper and more detailed approach to this rule, read *How to Win Friends and Influence People* by Dale Carnegie – it's considered the father of all self-improvement books by many.

Chapter 19
How to build rapid rapport and attraction

The next time you try to seduce anyone, don't do it with talk, with words. Women know more about words than men ever will. And they know how little they can ever possibly mean.

- William Faulkner

My Experience

Sunday afternoon.

I'm on my way to buy myself a scarf. It's getting cold as hell in Boston.

As I walk down Commonwealth Avenue, I'm secretly analyzing potential targets to approach. I figure I might as well get a girl to go with the scarf. I spot a fit looking girl in some tight yoga pants. She's wearing a pair of large bug-eye sunglasses (I think that's what those ginormous things are called).

She's sitting on a bench at the bus stop, listening to music. So I sit down beside her and lightly touch her shoulder to let her know I have a question. "What are you listening to? I'm in serious need of new music on my playlist."

"Ummmmm that's random. I'm listening to Pandora," she says with a confused looking smirk on her face.

"Duh! Well what station?" I reply while giving her a playful shove that turns her smirk into a full on smile.

We continue on for a few more minutes before I tell her I need to get going, give her my phone, and tell her to put her number in so that we can hang out (I find that this is a far better technique than just asking for it).

We ended up going on a date the next week, but as it turns out she was wearing the big ass sunglasses for a good reason.

Rule 19: Touch People

No words can build attraction as powerfully or efficiently as a well-placed touch.

Obviously the type of touching you can do is dependent on the situation. If you're at a bar, bringing her closer so she can hear you by placing your hand on her butt is acceptable. On the street, this could be perceived as a bit creepy. Something like touching her elbow while you compliment her shirt might work well, though.

Generally the hierarchy of touching (from least to most aggressive) is arm/shoulder, back, hips, and finally ass. Oh, I almost forgot to mention the easiest touch ever – the handshake. Always shake hands when you introduce yourself. One trick I use is holding the handshake (not shaking up and down, but just holding it) after the introduction. If she is comfortable, she will allow the hold to last for more than a few seconds. This also probably means she's attracted – so use this tactic.

While an alpha male obviously must be comfortable touching women socially, he must also be able to do so with his fellow men. A firm handshake and a congratulatory pat on the back are both displays of confidence and charisma.

Take Action

1. Shake 10 girls' hands, and hold the handshakes for as long as you can.
2. Touch 10 girls on the arm as you make small talk.
3. At the bar, touch 10 girls on the hips/butt while drawing them in closer.

Chapter 20
The dangers of obsession

If one oversteps the bounds of moderation, the greatest pleasures cease to please.

- Epictetus

My Experience

Midnight Friday.

I've just finished the second rewrite of my book. It's late, but I open up Photoshop to draft a cover image. I dread going to sleep without doing a little bit more work, making a little bit more progress...

I look at the bottom right hand corner of the computer screen – the clock reads 3 AM. I've begun and scrapped countless cover images. On one hand I feel obliged to continue into the wee hours of the morning. On the other, I'm beginning to feel sick and depressed.

I've stayed up every night over the past week until at least this time. Finishing the book has consumed my life. It's been a month since I've been out gaming or on a date, even. The gym hasn't alluded me yet, but my diet's been piss poor, and I haven't slept much.

The book has come a long way, yes – but I feel like shit. Yet I'm compelled to work on it, every free minute I have to myself.

Rule 20: Strike a Balance

When you allow one aspect of your life complete control, you ended up losing all control. It's some kind of paradox.

I've gone through this cycle with many different things. There was a period where I went out every Thursday, Friday, and Saturday night – and then also every Sunday through Wednesday afternoon or evening – to game girls. During that period, I was slaying the women, don't get me wrong, but my productivity at work and on my side-missions was non-existent.

Too much of anything is unhealthy - be it video games, drugs, food, sex, lifting weights, reading, or writing. In order to remain sane, productive, and healthy, the alpha male must strike a balance between the numerous competing interests and missions in his life. He must always have a hand in a number of different pots, and that hand should be active to some degree.

Take Action

1. List three or four missions you wish to focus on at this time. Circle your primary mission.
2. Schedule time in your week to tackle a few next actions for all of them. Allocate more time to the primary mission, but don't neglect the others altogether.

Chapter 21

An easy way to become the leader of any group

It does not take much strength to do things, but it requires great strength to decide on what to do.

- Elbert Hubbard

My Experience

Indecision is something I've struggled with since I was a youngster.

I can recall, like it was yesterday, being at the mall with my mom. Basketball season was about to start and I needed a new pairs of kicks. Basketball sneakers were like a second skin for me. As soon as I bought a new pair, I was entering into a long term relationship. I'd wear them to school, after school, to basketball practice, to basketball games, to church, on vacation – I would basically wear them everywhere I went over the next year. Needless to say, that day we went to the mall each year was a borderline religious ceremony for me.

After parking, we navigated our way to *Footlocker*. Upon entering, we were greeted by an overeager salesman – his peppy demeanor wouldn't last long. "Hi ma'am, I'm Doug, do you need a hand with any sneakers today?"

"Yes, my son needs a new pair of basketball shoes. He'll need to be measured; his toes have practically popped holes through the shoes on his feet."

The young man took out one of those oval-shaped metal foot measuring devices from under a bench, and instructed me to place my foot on one end. "He's about a six and a half or seven. We should have most of these in his size," he said while pointing to a nearby wall of basketball sneakers.

I was in heaven. Christmas had come early, once again. I spent five or ten minutes staring at the wall of paradise. "I want to try this one, this one, this one, and that one!"

Five minutes later Doug emerged juggling five or six shoe boxes. "We only had these in a six, but I brought a couple sizes out for all the others."

Over the next twenty minutes I tried on each pair and walked, ran, and jumped through the store – they needed to be thoroughly tested. "I like these two, but I don't know which one I want," I told my mom.

"Do you absolutely love either?" She asked.

"I don't know."

This back and forth goes on for ten minutes. "We're going to go for a walk so that my son can think about it," my mom told Doug, trying to get a breath of fresh air.

We walked around the mall, checked out a different store, and then continued the cycle. By the end of it my mom was about to kill me, and I was borderline crying out of indecision. Eventually I reluctantly made a choice, and we were out of there in an instant.

A feeling of communal relief filled the car on the drive home. Later that night I cuddled with the shoes in bed. The next morning I popped the cherry – lacing them up and showing them off at school. The decision itself never mattered, only that I'd made it.

Rule 21: Decide Quickly

Decision making is definitely a make-or-break characteristic of the alpha male. No matter how important or minute the situation, you must be able to make a quick choice, and take responsibility for whatever happens next – something that the common man is deathly afraid of.

If there's no obvious choice, then usually making an arbitrary decision is best – rarely does spending minutes, hours, or days thinking about something make much of a difference. And if it does, the benefits of the slightly improved decision are usually outweighed by the costs of delay, both tangible and to your decision-making confidence.

The most notable effect of stepping up and making repeated decisions, when in a group setting, is that you quickly become delegated as the decision maker of the group – and therefore the leader.

Take Action

1. Every time someone asks you to make a seemingly unimportant decision, like where to eat lunch or which outfit looks better, make an instant decision. The decision itself is not important.
2. Every time you're out at a restaurant, glance over the menu and make a choice within twenty seconds.

By practicing your decision making skills when there are little or no consequences, you build the habit and decision making power you need to execute similar haste and decisiveness in high risk situations.

Chapter 22

The only way to succeed

Energy and persistence conquer all things.

- Benjamin Franklin

My Experience

I finally took and passed my exam – I'm now a certified personal trainer.

A few months prior, my friend Mack told me about a high class gym that just opened in his neighborhood. I watched the video tour online and immediately fell in love. It looked more like a five star hotel than a gym. The equipment was flawless, the reception area had a fireplace, and the bathrooms were majestic. *I have to work here,* I thought. *If I'm to leave my software job, this is where I'll go.*

So I applied online. I didn't meet some of the credentials listed, such as holding bachelor's degree in exercise science or having two years of training experience. But this wasn't going to stop me from trying. I never heard back. So I called the gym, three or four times – each time the fitness manager was in a meeting or out of the office.

One evening on the way home from work I even stopped by to drop off my resume in person. When I arrived, there was a red carpet outside. As I approached the door, I was asked if my name was on the list. "What list?" I asked, shocked that you had to have your name on a list to enter the gym.

"Tonight we're holding a special cocktail party," the cute girl at the door informed me.

"I'm here to drop off my resume," I replied.

"You'll have to come back next week, sorry." I was crushed. Again, my advances had been rejected.

Giving it one last try, I came back the next week and dropped off my resume at the front desk. Again I was told that the fitness manager had gone home for the night. "I will make sure your resume lands on his desk," I was assured. But it didn't. Well, it probably did, but I never heard back. I didn't know how to proceed. I was out of ideas, but I had gotten my hopes up – I didn't want to continue going to my current job for 40-50 hours every week. I'd mentally checked out in anticipation of this new gig. *How should I proceed?*

On one Sunday afternoon, a few weeks later, my mom encouraged me to try one last time. "Fuck it! Why not?" I said. So I dialed the gym's number on my cell phone. The fitness manager was in! We spoke for ten minutes, and he agreed to give me a chance – I was to arrive at the gym that Thursday evening at six. The next four days went by very slowly, but I'd finally secured an interview – I was ecstatic.

Rule 22: Persist Indefinitely

If I hadn't persisted, I wouldn't have gotten the chance to work for my dream gym. The same persistence is what revolutionized my sex life and luck with women. If there's ever something you truly want in life, you must be prepared to face repeated failure on the path, and persist endlessly until you arrive at the gates.

The alpha male doesn't quit. He pushes on in the face of rejection. He is the last man standing.

Take Action

1. Choose your mission.
2. Define the next actions.
3. Go.
4. If circumstances change, re-evaluate the next actions – you will find a way, even if it means re-working the path over and over again.

Chapter 23
Don't be held back by the naysayers

Do not go where the path may lead, go instead where there is no path and leave a trail.

- Ralph Waldo Emerson

My Experience

It's 3PM on a Friday. I'm at the office. Today has taken an eternity to go by.

I was told I'd receive a call today with either an offer or a rejection. I've been waiting all day. No work has been done. I'm nervous. One on hand, I'm not sure if I will be extended an offer. I think so, but nothing is certain. On the other hand, it's going to be super awkward taking the call at my current job.

My parents, and most of my friends, have repeatedly questioned my decision. My current job is in line with everyone's expectations of my path in life. I recently received a promotion, which only further cemented their view that I should stay and continue to advance in the IT world. But I have a feeling that I cannot ignore – an itch that I absolutely need to scratch.

I have never been so sure of anything before in my life – and that says a lot, given my history of indecisiveness. If I'm extended an offer, I'll accept it on the spot. A work day of interacting with people face-to-face and helping them improve their fitness and overall health, something I truly care about, seems like a fantasy life to me – especially doing so in the luxury facilities that my prospective gym offers. My current work days involve sitting behind a computer, talking to clients on the phone, and sometimes traveling around the US to meet them in person. I go home every evening feeling drained and brain-dead. Nothing has ever been so black and white.

Over the past month I've endured an in person interview with the fitness manager, a session where I had to train one of the gym's current trainers, and an interview with the general manager. Everyone loved me, as far as I could tell. *Ugh, would he hurry up and call.* I just want to get ready for my new life's direction. I have no idea what I'll do in the event that I don't receive an offer – it's not a possibility I've allowed myself to think on.

Vrmmmm, Vrmmm, Vrmmmm. I feel my phone vibrate in my pocket. I answer. "Hello, this is David." It's the gym. This is the moment I've been not-so-patiently waiting for. "Give me a minute; I need to step outside the office." I walk to the nearest exit, and continue the conversation.

"David, I'm calling to formally extend you an offer to join my team." My heart begins to race. A smile emerges from ear-to-ear. *I fucking love myself – I did it!*

Rule 23: Create Your Own Path

In life, the people you grow close to, be it friends or family, will develop their own expectations of you. Most people cave in, consciously or unconsciously. They live the life that others want them to – but not the alpha.

The alpha chooses his own path, and decides to follow it, despite others' efforts to caution or altogether stop him. This happens in both a macro and a micro sense. The macro-sense is like my example above – it usually involves a large and deliberate decision, like changing careers or moving locations.

You won't miss these protests, but the micro-protests may fly under the radar. These usually involve subtle resistance to character changes and developments. For example, if someone isn't used to you making quick decisions, meditating, or following ambitious missions they will likely try to deter you from doing so. Yes, this seems like they're evil and trying to sabotage you, but that's not the case. Over time, they've developed certain expectations of who you are and they use this as a framework to relate to you. When their expectations don't match up with what you're doing in reality, they will do their best to change reality back to their expectations, both overtly and subconsciously.

As the alpha, you must stand strong and plow through this resistance.

Take Action

1. When you're following a mission or character change you've committed to, and someone close to you says or does something that makes it hard for you to continue on the new path, recognize it. Expect this to happen.
2. Explain to that person, in very clear language, that you've consciously and purposefully chosen to take on this new behavior or mission.
3. Ask them to offer you support. When you do so, tell them that you realize they may not understand your choice.

When you do this, one of two things will happen. They will either accept or reject your offer. If they accept it, great, they love you and understand that you need to do whatever it is that you're doing.

If they reject your offer or give you a hard time, they either don't understand, or they want to hold you back. Dig deeper, find out which it is, and proceed accordingly. If they don't understand, you may have to leave it at that, and ask that they accept the change anyway. If they seem to want to hold you back, it may be a good time to remove this person (or at least spending large amounts of time with this person) from your life.

Chapter 24

How to diffuse uncomfortable situations and move on with life

I think confrontation is healthy, because it clears the air very quickly.

- Bill Parcells

My Experience

It's the next day at work. I enter the office, nervous as hell.

I hope my boss is here so I can tell him that I'm quitting. *Do you have a few minutes to talk in private?* I've recited this to myself one hundred times in my head. I really hope he's already here so I can get it out of the way.

As I turn the corner to enter our area, my eyes dart to the corner of the room where he sits. *FUCK!* He's not here yet. I sit down. I don't even log onto my computer. I just sit there, and wait. Twenty minutes go by – still no sign of him. "Is Matt coming in today?" I ask the dude who sits on the other side of me.

"Yes, I think so."

After what seems like an eternity, he finally enters. I look at him. "Good morning, David," he says. I nod my head in acknowledgement but say nothing. *FUCK!* Why is this so hard?

A few minutes pass and I finally work up the nerve, "Matt, do you have a few minutes to talk in private?"

He spins in his chair and looks me in the eye. "Can we do it this afternoon? I have to get to a nine thirty meeting."

"Sure." I'm crushed, three or four more hours of this and I might have a heart attack. I get no work done over the next three and a half hours – it seems like an eternity, again.

After lunch, Matt approaches my cubicle, "You good to go?" We walk into a nearby conference room and sit down.

I pause for a second, look him in the eye, and say, "I wanted to tell you that I've decided to change careers. It's nothing about the job here – you guys have been great to me and facilitated a lot of personal growth. It's just that I want to try something new." I sit and wait.

"Ok," he begins, "do you mind if I ask where you're going?" There's no sign of anger or resentment on his face. He isn't upset, and barely even surprised. *That wasn't so bad at all.*

Rule 24: Confront when Necessary

I went through this same experience when I asked for a raise. I go through a similar, albeit not as intense, experience every time I have to confront one of my close friends about something personal, that I feel might upset them. Approaching random girls on the street or at the bar is also similar.

Many people allow their nerves and fears to get the best of them and never actually go through with any of these things, be it approaching a girl or asking for a raise. The alpha is different. He recognizes that he must do so to advance on his journey. He acknowledges that it won't be easy to do it, but he proceeds anyway – because it must be done.

Take Action

1. Next time you find yourself in an uncomfortable situation where you must approach or confront someone, recognize it.
2. Identify the worst possible outcome – usually this is rejection or upsetting someone.
3. Accept the possibility of this outcome.
4. Knowing that you can't proceed as you want to in life without making the confrontation, go ahead and do it – as soon as possible. It's best to get these things out of the way.

Refer to the *Take Action* section of the *Face the Fear of Failure* chapter for a series of activities to practice this rule right now.

Chapter 25

Don't be limited by your own experience

Always assume you are the least intelligent person in the room.

- James Altucher

My Experience

I sat down in the chair. It was a Saturday afternoon, and I'd just arrived at the barber shop.

"What can I do you for?" the barber asked me. My regular lady didn't work weekends, so I was stuck with a new barber. He was average height, with black slicked back hair, and a full sleeve tattoo on his right arm. It looked like a dragon or something mystical. I love cool tattoos.

"Bring it down to about a three on the sides, leave the length on top, and blend it with scissors," I instructed.

He began his work. "Are you a college student?"

"No, I went to school around here, but I'm out now." The boring small talk continued for a bit.

"I have a question for you," I said. "When I shave I always tend to maul the skin beneath my jawline. How do you shave, personally?" His eyes lit up. I could tell he had a passion for what he did.

"Aww, of course," he began his speech. "Well the most important thing is the razor. If the blade is dull, you'll definitely cut yourself, and won't even get a good shave."

"Guilty as charged," I replied. "I definitely notice a better shave when I have a fresh blade, but even then I tend to cut myself up."

He laughed, and was quick to continue my education. "Another common mistake people make is the direction in which they shave."

I interjected, "With the grain, right?"

"Nope!" He corrected me, with a smirk on his face. "Most people make that same mistake. If you shave against the grain, you'll be a bloody mess. If you shave with the grain, you'll never get close. You must shave diagonally across the grain," he instructed me as he motioned his right index finger across his cheek. I could tell he was enjoying himself. And so was I – after all, there was a chance I would no longer murder myself every time I shaved.

"If you do that, half the battle is won. Do you shave right after your shower, in a steamy bathroom?" He asked.

"Yes, I got that much right," I responded.

"Good, good." He walked over to the mirror and traded the clippers for a long pair of scissors. "My final shaving secret is *Noxzema.*"

I cut him off, "The thing chicks use to wash their faces?"

He laughed. "Indeed. Apply a thin layer of *Noxzema* on your skin before shaving – you'll thank me later."

He was right. The next morning I applied *Noxzema* and shaved diagonally across the grain. It was the closest, smoothest, and least-bloody shave of my life. Thank you, Mr. Barber.

Rule 25: Learn From Everyone

The alpha is proud, but he doesn't let pride get in the way of his education. He realizes that everyone is smarter than him, in some respect. He takes advantage of this by extracting the relevant knowledge out of everyone he speaks with.

This also falls in line with the previous law, *Take an Interest in Others*. Areas of extreme interest tend to be areas where that person is more knowledgeable than you. One example is asking the barber about shaving. On one hand he knows so much about shaving that he was able to offer valuable information to me. On the other hand, he loves talking about shaving, so he really enjoyed our conversation.

Another example came when I started working at the gym. The experienced personal trainers at my gym loved training, and had been doing it for years. I was new, so I spent my first few weeks picking their brains. By asking them about their respective training styles I learned a lot that I was able to apply myself, and I also built solid rapport with each of them in the process.

Take Action

Call up a friend right now and do the following. Also do the same with all friends, family, and strangers going forward.

1. Focus your conversation on an area of expertise of the other person. Preferably something you know little about.
2. Listen actively, and ask questions to pry further and further into this area.
3. Use this opportunity to learn new things.

David De Las Morenas

Chapter 26
A recipe for earning respect

I'm not in this world to live up to your expectations and you're not in this world to live up to mine.

- Bruce Lee

My Experience

"David, I'm going to send an email out to corporate, recognizing your second month at the club," my boss tells me.

"What for?" I ask – I'm confused.

"You sold over $7,000 of training. I gave you a goal of $2,000 and wasn't sure you'd hit it," he explains. "You straight up murdered it, and I want to give you proper recognition."

A warm feeling moves over my body. "Thank you."

I wasn't really aware of the sales goal, I'll be honest. Everything was still so new to me. I had simply tried to do as many sessions and sell as much training as I possibly could. I thought I was doing all right, but had no idea that I had exceeded my goal by that much. There were still plenty of sales I lost and members I never approached. I was just about in line with my own expectations, I'd say.

A few days later I got the email. I was cc'd on it. It praised my strong start and asked me to reply with the three key ingredients I could attribute my early success to. I replied with *persistence, patience,* and *the team* (everything the other trainers had taught me).

Over the course of the next few days, one-by-one, most of the other trainers gave me props. I even received a few emails from the higher-up corporate folk. It felt good. I enjoyed the recognition, although it all seemed like a bit much. The most valuable thing I received as a result of this situation was undoubtedly the increased respect from the other trainers. I was no longer the *new guy*. I was now on their level, and in some cases, someone to look up to.

Rule 26: Exceed Expectations

When all was said and done, the main lesson I learned from this experience was the value of exceeding others' expectations.

Unfortunately, most people tend to under-deliver and constantly fail to meet what's expected of them. The alpha male is an exception to this rule. Whether it's completing a project well ahead of the deadline, destroying a sales goal, or just giving someone your full and undivided attention every time you see them, people will notice. They will become drawn to your excellence. They will develop an overwhelming respect for you.

Take Action

1. Take pride in everything you do.
2. Make it your mission to over-deliver in whatever activity you're currently involved in.
3. If you fail to over-deliver, that's fine. Failure is inevitable, but chances are you at least met their expectations, even if you

fell short of your own. You can rest easy, knowing that the intention was there.

Chapter 27
Why this one mistake will kill your game

Only strength can cooperate. Weakness can only beg.

- Dwight D. Eisenhower

My Experience

"David, there's something we need to talk about." I'm hanging out with a girl that I've been hooking up with consistently for the last two months. "What are we doing?" She asks.

She's finally popped the question – a question that single men both love and hate at the same time. The question is of course *can we become exclusive boyfriend and girlfriend*. We love it because we've successfully attracted a girl who likes us so much that she wants to lock us down. It makes us feel proud – like we've done our job. We hate it because we must either commit to a long term relationship, or give up the sex we've been enjoying as of late.

But that's all beside the point. I've never officially dated a girl before. At times I wanted a girlfriend. Those were the times I always had no luck, not even hooking up with girls. Other times, I just wanted to go out and have fun – or was looking for a hookup, but nothing more. Those were the times I would kill it. That's where I am now, and thus this question is one I don't want to answer. And so I put it off, as I always have. "I don't know, let's go get some food."

But she brought it up again two weeks later. *Stubborn girl,* I thought. This time I accepted her advance. I'd thought about it, and decided to give the whole *girlfriend* thing a try, and see what it was all about. After making it through all of college, and avoiding the girlfriend trap, maybe it was time to test it out.

Honestly, so far it's been great. I've dated this girl for the past six months, and enjoyed every minute of it. Her femininity is refreshing, and I love the time I spend with her.

Rule 27: Don't Look for a Girlfriend

The alpha isn't needy.

It doesn't matter if you want a girlfriend or not. The fact is that if you do, and this idea is present in your mind when you're out meeting girls or hooking up with one, it will manifest itself in your actions. She will sense your desire for her – she will sense your longing. This tends to turn women off, because they want things they can't have. They want a man they can't tame. They want one that's a challenge to lock down – one that puts his life missions over his women.

The outright desire for a long term relationship will spoil your game. It will bleed through in your words and your body language. Even if you do manage to hook up with and maybe even begin dating a girl while using this mindset, there's a chance it will ruin the relationship. Successful relationships are based upon a strong masculine vs. feminine dynamic. The man must be in control. He must lead the course of the journey. If you start a relationship on the basis of you chasing her, this dynamic is all but ruined.

Take Action

1. If you desire a girlfriend, set that desire aside. You don't have to convince yourself that you don't want a girlfriend, only that you aren't looking for one at this very moment in time.

2. Approach girls with the mindset that you simply want to meet them and have fun.

Chapter 28
How bragging will sabotage your reputation

Sense shines with a double luster when it is set in humility. An able yet humble man is a jewel worth a kingdom.

- William Penn

My Experience

I was meeting a new client for the first time. He was only the second or third client I had trained thus far at the new job. After discussing his goals, reviewing his health history, and laying out a plan – I took a moment to let him know that I had recently published a book.

"David, what do I need to do to cut fat?" he asked me.

"Diet is most important. You must create a caloric deficit in order to shed bodyweight," I explained.

After thinking for a minute, he asked, "I see, and what about eating late at night?"

I smiled. "That's not important in regard to weight loss. I actually just published a book that explains the science behind the various processes that affect body composition," I told him. Then I waited, expecting praise and awe.

"Oh, cool." That was his response. No follow up question – nothing. He had literally no interest in reading my book. Compare that reaction with the following story.

I'm at a party with a few of the other trainers from my gym. "Yo, Dave," one of them says. "Some dude with the same name as you published a book."

I look at him. "What?" I'm confused. *Does he mean my book?*

"I was browsing bodybuilding books on Amazon and there's a guy, David De Las Morenas, who published a book on bodybuilding - simple bodybuilding or something like that," he stops and waits for my response.

"Yeah, that's me."

Now he's looking at me with a confused look on his face. "Don't fuck with me."

I laugh, "No really, I wrote that."

The rest of the night he told everyone at the party about my book. "Sorry if I'm being a huge fan boy right now," he said later on in the night.

I found it all very funny, especially because this guy is a beast. He's like 6'3" and competes in bodybuilding shows. He hadn't spoken to me much before then, either. Now I think he loves me.

Rule 28: Remain Humble

The two different reactions above demonstrate the powerful negative effects of bragging. It doesn't matter if you just landed on the moon and banged Jessica Alba – when you announce it at the top of your lungs as you enter the room, it falls on deaf ears. Worse, people may treat you in a dismissive fashion.

As you change and grow, you will undoubtedly accomplish impressive feats. While most men fail to contain their excitement and keep their cool, the alpha doesn't succumb to social pressure. He doesn't feel the need to prove himself to others with self-praise. His confidence and presence are evident enough through his body language, speech, and mannerisms. Furthermore, when people inevitably learn of your successes and escapades on their own, or from someone else, a far larger impression is made than bragging could ever produce.

Take Action

1. Keep your triumphs to yourself.

2. If you're asked directly about it or it comes up naturally in conversation, then feel free to mention it, but don't lose your cool. Keep it brief. The other party will hammer away with questions if they're intrigued.

Chapter 29
A method for dealing with the inevitable bad days

Each thing is of like form from everlasting and comes round again in its cycle.

- Marcus Aurelius

My Experience

I'm sitting in traffic, my hands are freezing, my throat is sore, and I desperately need to take a poop – after this morning I'm guessing it's more diarrhea.

At this pace I'm going to be late for my four o'clock training session with Joe, one of my older clients. After him I have four more – all back to back. Moreover, I'm starving and haven't eaten since breakfast, because I got caught up in a messy project for my software job this afternoon (I now work part-time from home, by the way – they offered me this position after I quit). I'll have to wait until nine for dinner. *Fuck my life.*

These are just the immediate circumstances. I've been losing clients left-and-right over the past few weeks, I'm not on pace to hit my sales goal for the quarter, and my recent effort to grow my fitness blog (www.BornToBulk.com) via YouTube has yielded zero results. Add all of this to the fact that my strength has inexplicably dropped on my squat and bench press, and now you have a good picture of just how shitty I feel today.

Rule 29: Expect the Lows

This was two weeks ago (from the time of me writing this chapter). Since then I've picked up a couple new clients, regained lost strength and then some, and been in a great overall mood. I've also written a lot of this book!

Life is cyclical. We all go through periods of ups and downs. While many people let the down cycles ruin their moods, and succumb to the negativity, the alpha male does not. When things aren't going his way – he gets sick, a family member dies, or some other bad shit happens – he accepts the circumstances and takes a step back. He patiently waits for the up-cycle to come back around.

Furthermore, he takes advantage of the down cycle by relaxing and taking his foot off the gas pedal, allowing his missions to stagnate while he regains composure. Then, when things start going his way, he presses back down and crushes everything in his path.

Take Action

1. When a series of seemingly bad events or circumstances come your way, recognize it.
2. Give yourself a few days or even a week of rest from all but the most essential work. Don't worry about the next actions or the pending missions.
3. Get more sleep, eat a healthy diet, meditate, and read.

The combination of less work with more rest and recovery will shorten the down cycle and give you the oomph you need to kill it when things come back around.

Chapter 30

How to be happy with what you have while still striving for more

Be happy, but never satisfied.

- Bruce Lee

My Experience

Lately I've had the urge to move. I'm living with two roommates in Boston right now.

I want to move somewhere warm for a year or two. I've spent almost my whole life in snowy, cold Boston. I'm thinking southern California or southern Spain. That would be perfect. I would wake up every day and go to work in short sleeves and shorts. The heating bill wouldn't crush my bank account each month. I would be on the beach whenever I wanted.

I could get a place of my own: I had one before this and then changed back to roommates – a terrible choice. It's only a bit cheaper, but I have to deal with their dirty dishes and different sleep patterns.

I would be so much happier.

And that's where I caught myself. I incorporated a new habit into my life a few months ago, while reading *Choose Yourself* by James Altucher (another great book). Every morning when I wake up, I take a few minutes to list five things I'm grateful for. I name things from friends and family members, to my job and my health. Today I listed Boston – and my roommates.

I'm grateful to live in such a thriving city. Boston is full of young people. It has a great nightlife. It has an unlimited number of daytime attractions too – from the nature of the Boston Commons to the super cool exhibits at the Museum of Science. It also has the amazing gym that I absolutely love to go to work at every afternoon – all of this, right at my fingertips.

I'm thankful to have such awesome roommates. We all pitch in with cleaning, taking the trash out, shoveling the snow, and other house duties. I love hanging out with them several nights a week and shooting the shit or watching a basketball game. I love going out to the bars with them on occasion, or grabbing burritos down the street.

Life is good. I'm grateful to live in Boston with my roommates.

Rule 30: Be Grateful

It's all too easy to get caught up in the endless cycle of wanting more. Ambition is good, yes – but a certain type of ambition. The alpha male has missions he means to accomplish, that will advance him on his life journey. At the same time he must accept his current circumstances. More than that, really – he should be grateful for, and even love his current circumstances.

When all you do is want more, you place yourself in a position of lacking. You begin to feel incompetent, despite the probability that you've accomplished a number of important missions in your life. It's human nature to want a new car, a new TV, a new job, or a new girlfriend – and you may legitimately be better off with one of these things. But it's important to be thankful for the current circumstances. Only once you accept and show gratitude for them will you be able to advance from a place of confidence and resourcefulness.

Take Action

1. Right now, and every morning going forward, list five things that you have right now that you're grateful for.

Can You Do Me A Favor?

Thank you so much for taking the time to read my book. If you enjoyed it or found it useful, please leave me a review on Amazon, because I want it to help as many men as possible. That would be awesome. Thank you again.

About the Author

David is a writer, engineer, and personal trainer living in Boston. After graduating college, he initially began a career as a software engineer, which he soon left to pursue a series of missions that have begun to define his life. You can follow him on his blog: www.HowToBeast.com.

Made in the USA
San Bernardino, CA
09 May 2015